CHOP, COOK, MUNCH!

**Fun, Fast & Fresh
Recipes
for Young Chefs**

by Janet Burgess

AuthorHouse™
1663 Liberty Drive
Bloomington, IN 47403
www.authorhouse.com
Phone: 1-800-839-8640

First published by AuthorHouse 05/05/2012

ISBN: 978-1-4772-0429-0 (sc)

Library of Congress Control Number: 2012908169

Printed in the United States of America

This book is printed on acid-free paper.

authorHOUSE®

This book is dedicated to the Julia's in my life:
My mother, Julia Chelberg, who taught me about nutrition
and making meals come together as a family.

And to the Godmother of many American cooks,
Julia Child, who demanded to know many years ago
why I hadn't written a cookbook.

Julia, here it is.

Acknowledgements

Carole Stolte Upman, Chesapeake Disability Management, Inc.

Cristina Coletti Menegatti, Conegliano, Italy

Ariela Wilcox of the Wilcox Agency

David Davis of MCD Advertising and Design

Table of Contents

Introduction

Hi, Kids!

This cookbook is for you with a little help from an adult in some of the recipes. Get ready to have a cooking adventure while learning to measure, scoop, beat, mix and have fun cooking healthy food. You will learn that reading the recipe first and getting your equipment and food together is a very important step as we get ready to cook. Make breakfast dishes, luscious lunches, yummy dinners, fun desserts and super snacks. You will develop new and exciting skills and learn about the safe, fun way to create wonderful food for you and your family. One of the most important things you can do while learning about cooking is to remember some important things about eating. You need lots of fruits and vegetables every day. You also need to make half the grains you eat whole grains, like whole grain cereals, breads and oatmeal. Try to incorporate the Famous Fourteen Foods that are listed in this book in your diet everyday. They are totally yummy and create strong bones and give you lots of energy. Remember to start your day with dairy foods like milk and yogurt. And don't forget to get moving! The lessons you will learn about eating well will carry you through a lifetime of making smart choices about food and nutrition.

Hi, Adult Helpers!

The following recipes have been kid tested numerous times. When recipes list that a knife is required; the knife can be a plastic disposable knife. It will work just fine for cutting veggies, fruits, breads, etc. When hot mitts are required to place or remove an item from the oven, it's also listed in the recipe. When children grow up with a large variety of food their palate is awakened to the wonderful taste of many different flavors.

Experiencing these flavors and varieties of food will help them make better choices as they grow. If you're someone who enjoys the magical world of children, these delicious recipes will remind you of the cooking adventures of the kitchen.

Happy Cooking!

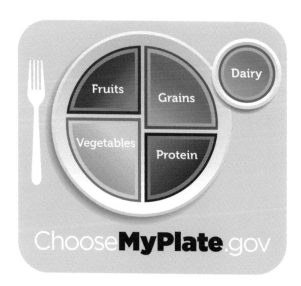

ChooseMyPlate.gov

The United States Department of Agriculture recommends the following changes to our American lifestyle when it comes to food choices:

- Lean Proteins rather than fatty or processed choices

- Reduce sodium intake to no more than 1,500 units a day

- Increase your fish intake for more omega 3 fatty acids

- Eat more fruits and vegetables and healthy nuts

- Upgrade your carbohydrate intake with whole grains

Kitchen Math

3 teaspoons = 1 tablespoon

4 tablespoons = ¼ cup

5 tablespoons + 1 teaspoon = 1/3 cup

8 tablespoons = ½ cup

16 tablespoons = 1 cup

1 cup = ½ pint = 8 liquid ounces

2 cups = 1 pint = 16 liquid ounces

2 pints = 4 cups = 32 liquid ounces = 1 quart

4 quarts =128 liquid ounces = 1 gallon

Dash = a few sprinkles

Famous Fourteen Foods

Everyone should eat some of the foods from this list everyday to stay healthy and have lots of energy:

Beans	Oranges	Spinach	Walnuts
Blueberries	Pumpkin	Tea	Yogurt
Broccoli	Wild Salmon	Tomatoes	
Oats	Soy	Turkey	

Start Your Engines!

- Read through the entire recipe

- Gather all the equipment needed

- Assemble all the ingredients

- Follow the recipe step by step

Safety Tips for the Kitchen

- Find an adult who can help you. Always read through the recipe with your adult helper so you can ask questions about the recipe or equipment.

- Wash your hands with soap and water. Sing happy birthday to yourself for several verses to make sure your hands are clean. If you touch your hair or face, wash your hands again.

- Wear an apron to keep your clothes clean. Don't wear shirts with long, loose sleeves. If your hair is long, pull it back into a ponytail.

- Keep a damp cloth or paper towel nearby to clean up spills.

- Always use hot mitts to handle hot items from the stove, oven or microwave.

- Know where your first aid kit is located. If you touch something hot, run your hands under cold water immediately.

- Always pick up a knife or kitchen scissors by the handle. Leave sharp items on the counter until you are ready to wash them. Don't put them in soapy water; you might reach in and cut yourself.

- Wear shoes that are close-toed in the kitchen, as knives or scissors may fall from the counter.

- When cooking on the stove, turn handles of the pans and skillets toward the middle or back of the stove, so you won't bump handles and spill hot food.

Measuring Ingredients

- Dry Ingredients: Items like flour, sugar, oatmeal, grains are measured in a nested-type measuring cup or measuring spoon. Dip measuring cup into the flour or canister to get it heaping full. Be sure to level off the top of the measuring cup with a knife.

- Liquid Measure: Liquids like water, milk, oil and broth are measured in a measuring cup. Place cup on a table. Pour in liquid to proper mark. Bend down and look at the mark at eye level to make sure it's correct.

Let's Get Started on a Cooking Adventure!

Kid-Pleasing Breakfasts

Large bowl

Small bowl
(microwave-safe)

Measuring cup

Measuring spoons

Large mixing spoon

Jelly roll pan

Hot mitts

You can have this granola with milk or yogurt for breakfast or serve in a flat-bottomed ice cream cone for a snack.

Oatmeal Granola Crunch

Makes 7 servings

Directions:

1. Preheat oven to 350°.

2. For Syrup: Melt the butter in a microwave-safe dish for 30 seconds. Stir in honey, cinnamon and vanilla. Mix well.

3. For Granola: In a large bowl combine the oats, almonds, coconut sunflower seeds and salt.
Pour syrup mixture over the granola ingredients. Stir until well mixed.

4. Evenly spread the granola in the pan. Bake in oven for 30 minutes, stirring mixture after 15 minutes.

5. Remove from oven using hot mitts. When mixture is cooled, add the dried cherries and blueberries.

Ingredients

3 cups rolled oats
2/3 cup sliced almonds
¾ cup sweetened shredded
    coconut

1/3 cup sunflower seeds
½ teaspoon salt
1 cup dried blueberries
1 cup dried cherries

Syrup:
½ stick (¼ cup) unsalted
    butter, melted
6 tablespoons honey
½ teaspoon cinnamon
½ teaspoon vanilla extract

Tools

Cutting board
Knife
Blender
Measuring cups
Serving cups

Outrageous Orange Banana and Blueberry Smoothies

Makes 2 servings

Directions:

1. Peel bananas, break into chunks. Place into blender.

2. Measure out frozen blueberries and place in blender.

3. Add orange juice and ice cubes. Cover and pulse in blender until well blended.

4. Pour into cups and serve.

You can also use 2 cups chopped strawberries instead of the bananas. You can also substitute one cup of plain yogurt for one cup of orange juice.

Ingredients

2 bananas
1 cup frozen blueberries
2 cups orange juice
2 ice cubes

7

Lemon Cranberry Sour Cream Muffins

Directions:

1. Preheat oven to 350°.

2. Place muffin liners in muffin pan.

3. Stir together flour, baking soda, salt, cinnamon and sugar in a large bowl.

4. Use fork to beat egg in a small bowl.

5. Combine egg and sour cream.

6. Melt butter in a microwave-safe dish for 30 seconds. Cool.

7. Add butter and milk to the egg and sour cream. Mix well.

8. Combine egg mixture and flour mixture. Add cranberries.

9. With a grater, grate only the yellow part of the lemon. Add to mixture and stir briefly, leaving lumps in batter. Too much mixing will make the batter tough.

10. Spoon mixture into muffin cups.

11. Bake for 20 to 25 minutes.

12. Remove from oven using hot mitts.

13. Let muffins cool slightly before serving.

Tools

Muffin liners and pan
Large bowl
Small bowl

Microwave-safe dish
Grater
Measuring cups
Measuring spoons

Mixing spoon
Fork
Hot mitts

Ingredients

1 cup all purpose flour
1 teaspoon baking soda
¼ teaspoon salt

¼ teaspoon cinnamon
1/3 cup sugar
1 egg, slightly beaten
¼ cup sour cream

2 tablespoons unsalted butter, melted
¼ cup milk
½ cup dried cranberries
Zest of one lemon

9

Pie pan

Blender

Cutting board

Small knife

Spatula

Measuring cups

Hot mitts

Eggalicious Ham Breakfast Pie

Makes 6 to 8 servings

Directions:

1. Preheat oven to 350°.

2. Spray pie pan with non-stick spray. Tear bread into pieces, place in blender, cover and pulse until blended into crumbs. Pour crumbs into pan and tilt from side to side to cover bottom and sides completely with crumbs.

3. Use a knife to cut bacon into ¼ inch strips on cutting board; cut strips crosswise into ¼ inch squares. Sprinkle bacon and mozzarella cheese into pan.

4. Place parsley, cottage cheese, and eggs in blender, cover and pulse until well blended.

5. Pour into pan on top of bacon and cheese, scraping out blender with a spatula. Smooth top of pie with spatula.

6 Bake for about 35 minutes, until pie is golden and a knife blade inserted comes out clean.

7. Remove pie from oven using hot mitts and let stand 5 minutes before serving.

Ingredients

Non-stick spray for pie pan
1 slice whole wheat bread
1 cup Canadian bacon, cut into strips

1 cup shredded mozzarella cheese
1 sprig of fresh parsley leaves
2 cups lowfat cottage cheese
3 eggs

Waffle iron

Non-stick spray
for waffle iron

Large mixing bowl

Small bowl

Fork

Measuring cups

Measuring spoons

Spatula

Hot mitts

Nutty Pumpkin Waffles

Makes 8 servings

Directions:

1. Spray waffle iron lightly with non-stick spray.

2. Combine flour, baking powder, salt, cinnamon, nutmeg and pumpkin spice together in a large bowl.

3. In a small bowl, mix eggs with a fork.

4. Combine the eggs with milk, oil and pumpkin. Add to the dry ingredients and mix well.

5. Pour batter onto a hot waffle iron. Sprinkle with a few chopped nuts and bake until done.

Ingredients

2-½ cups all purpose flour
4 teaspoons baking powder
½ teaspoon salt

¾ teaspoon ground cinnamon
¼ teaspoon ground nutmeg
½ teaspoon pumpkin spice
2 egg yolks

1 ¾ cups milk
½ cup vegetable oil
½ cup canned pumpkin puree
¾ cup chopped pecan pieces

Tools

1 large bowl

1 medium bowl

Measuring cups

Measuring spoons

Muffin pan

Muffin liners

Grater

Spatula

Large spoon

Hot mitts

"Pick Your Fruit" Mighty Muffins

Makes 12 muffins

Directions:

1. Preheat oven to 400°.

2. In a large bowl, combine flours, baking soda and salt; mix well.

3. In a medium bowl, combine milk, eggs, honey and oil.

4. Add dry ingredients to the milk mixture. Stir until all the ingredients are moistened and add raisins.

5. Mash a banana or grate an apple or pear to mix into the ingredients. Make sure you only use one type of fruit.

6. Stir all the ingredients until blended.

7. Using a large spoon put the batter into the muffin cups, filling about 3/4 full.

8. Bake 18 to 20 minutes or until golden brown. Remove from oven using hot mitts.

Ingredients

1-½ cups all purpose flour
½ cup whole wheat flour
1 tablespoon baking soda
½ teaspoon salt

2/3 cup milk
2 eggs
¼ cup honey
¼ cup vegetable oil

1 cup raisins
1 medium grated apple,
or 1 medium mashed banana,
or 1 medium pear, grated

Serrated knife

Spoon

Small bowl

Measuring spoons

Measuring cups

Shallow bowl

Skillet

Platter

Aluminum foil

Strawberry Jam Sauce:

Combine 1 cup of strawberry jam with ¼ cup water, mix well. Serve over French toast.

Totally Stuffed French Toast

Directions:

Makes 8 slices

1. Cut the bread into 8 slices, 1 ½ inches wide. Cut a pocket into each slice by cutting the top of the bread crust, almost to the bottom, with a serrated bread knife. Do not cut all the way through to the bottom of the slice.

2. Combine the cream cheese, strawberries, banana, vanilla extract and jam in a small bowl to make the filling for the pocket. Place a large tablespoon of filling into each pocket, pressing together carefully.

3. Beat the eggs and milk in a shallow bowl. Place the bread into the bowl and let it coat the bread for a minute. Turn the bread over with a spatula and coat the other side.

4. Heat 2 tablespoons of the butter in a large skillet or non-stick pan. Add the some of the bread slices, but don't crowd the pan. Cook until the bread is light brown, turn and cook the other side.

5. Remove the bread from the pan and place on a platter or serving dish. Cover with foil to keep warm. Place the leftover butter in the skillet and cook the remaining pieces of bread.

Ingredients

1 loaf of French or challah bread, about 12 inches long
4 ounces of cream cheese, softened

¼ cup chopped strawberries
¼ cup chopped banana
½ teaspoon vanilla extract
2 tablespoons strawberry jam
6 eggs, lightly beaten

¾ cup milk
3 tablespoons unsalted butter, divided use
Strawberry jam sauce

Wire whisk

Non-stick skillet

Squeeze bottle

Non-stick pan spray

Spatula

Personalized Pancakes

Makes 12-14 pancakes

Directions:

1. Using a whisk, blend baking mix, milk, eggs and mashed fruit until smooth. Place batter in squeeze bottle.

2. Spray the skillet with non-stick spray and heat over a medium flame.

3. Using squeeze bottle, write your name, initials or a heart in the center of the pan. You must write them backwards because when you flip the pancake they will be facing you in reverse.

4. Cook as usual until bubbles form and the edges are cooked, and then flip.

What you see is what you wrote in the pancake.

These are especially nice for Mother's Day and Father's Day.

Ingredients

2 cups of multi-grain or low-fat baking mix

1 cup milk

2 eggs

¾ cup fruit such as mashed banana or mashed berries

Sweet Cinnamon Puffs

Directions:

Makes 16 puffs

Large bowl

Measuring cups

Measuring spoons

Pastry blender or two knives

Fork

Cutting board

Microwave-safe bowl

Small shallow bowl

Hot mitts

1. Preheat oven to 450°.

2. Stir flour, baking powder, salt in a large bowl.

3. Add the shortening to the flour mixture using a pastry blender or cutting the shortening into the mix with two knives. The mixture should be crumbly.

4. Stir in the milk using a fork. Stir until the dough holds together and makes into a ball. Turn the dough onto a lightly floured cutting board.

5. Roll the dough ball around several times. Knead the dough lightly by folding, pressing down and turning it. Repeat about 15 times until the dough is smooth.

6. Divide the dough into 16 pieces. Roll each piece into a smooth ball. Place dough on ungreased baking sheet. Bake for 10-12 minutes.

7. Melt the butter in a microwave-safe bowl for 30 seconds.

8. Mix the sugar and cinnamon together in a small bowl.

9. Remove puffs from oven using hot mitts. While puffs are still warm, remove from the baking sheet and roll each one in melted butter, then roll in the cinnamon sugar mixture.

Ingredients

2 cups all purpose flour
3 teaspoons baking powder
½ teaspoon salt
¼ cup shortening

¾ cup milk
1/3 cup unsalted butter
½ cup sugar
2 teaspoons cinnamon

15

Tea Party Apricot Scones

Makes 12 scones

Tools

Food processor

Grater

Large bowl

Fork

Cutting board

Baking sheet

Non-stick spray

Hot mitts

Directions:

1. Preheat oven to 350°.

2. Spray baking sheet with non-stick spray.

3. Using a hand grater, grate orange zest, making sure to use the orange part only.

4. In a large bowl mix flour, sugar, baking powder, salt, orange zest, shortening, egg and milk. Mix in the diced apricots.

5. Place dough on a floured cutting board and knead gently until dough is smooth.

6 Divide the dough in half and make each portion into a ¾ inch round disk. Cut each disk into 6 wedges and place on a baking sheet, keeping one inch between the scones.

7. Bake until they are golden brown, 18-20 minutes.

8. Remove from oven using hot mitts. Cool slightly and serve with apricot jam or honey.

Ingredients

2 cups all purpose flour
½ cup sugar
1 tablespoon baking powder

¼ teaspoon salt
1 teaspoon orange zest
2 tablespoons vegetable shortening

1 egg
½ cup milk
¾ cup chopped dried apricots

South of the Border Breakfast Tacos

Makes 3 servings

Directions:

1. In a medium bowl, combine eggs and milk. Beat well and add salt and pepper.

2. Spray the skillet with non-stick spray.

3. Pour in egg mixture, stirring constantly over medium high heat. Cook eggs to desired firmness.

4. Add ham strips and cheese and cook until just heated through.

5. Wrap tortillas in a damp paper towel and microwave for 30 seconds.

6. Spoon egg mixture into tortillas and roll up.

7. Serve with salsa.

Lip Smacking Lunches

Tools

Can opener

Food processor

Measuring cups

Measuring spoons

Spatula

Knife

Baking sheet

Hot mitts

Healthy Pita Pizzas with Homemade Hummus

Makes 4 servings

Directions:

1. Preheat oven to 425°.

2. Combine garbanzos, oil, juice, garlic, tahini sauce, salt and pepper in a food processor or blender. Pulse until mixture is smooth.

3. Spread the garbanzo mixture on pita bread rounds; place chopped tomato, cucumber slices and cheese on top of pita.

4. Bake for 8-10 minutes or until cheese is lightly browned. Remove from oven using hot mitts.

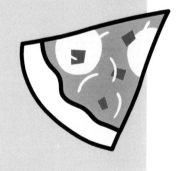

Did you know that pizzas are over 3,000 years old? The word "pizza" is related to "pita" and food history indicates pizzas were made by the ancient Egyptians.

Ingredients

1 can (15 ounces) garbanzo beans, rinsed and drained
3 tablespoons extra virgin olive oil

2 teaspoons lemon juice
1 clove minced garlic
2 tablespoons tahini sauce
½ teaspoon salt
¼ teaspoon black pepper

4 pita bread rounds
1 cup chopped tomato
1 cup sliced cucumbers
1 ½ cups shredded cheddar cheese

Large bowl

Small bowl

Can opener

Strainer

Measuring cups

Measuring spoons

Small knife

Cutting board

Yummy Chicken Taco Coleslaw

Makes 6 servings

Directions:

1. Open bags of coleslaw and place ingredients in a large bowl.

2. Add rinsed and drained black beans, cilantro, frozen corn, onions, tomatoes and chicken to the bowl.

3. Sprinkle salad with BBQ seasoning. Cut lime in two and squeeze lime over entire salad

4. In a separate bowl, combine the Caesar dressing and salsa.

5. Mix with coleslaw in large bowl. Serve in a large lettuce leaf.

Ingredients

2 bags of coleslaw

1 can (15 ounces) black beans, rinsed and drained

½ cup chopped cilantro

2/3 cup frozen corn

1 cup grape or cherry tomatoes, halved

1 cup cooked boneless chicken, chopped in one inch pieces

3 green onions, chopped

1 teaspoon BBQ seasoning

1 lime

½ cup Caesar dressing

½ cup store bought salsa

Paper towels
Parchment paper
Baking sheet
Small knife
Hot mitts

Ham, Cheese and Arugula Quesadillas

Makes 6 servings

Directions:

1. Preheat oven to 375°.

2. Heat tortillas in a microwave, wrapped in damp paper towel, for one minute.

3. Place shredded cheese, ham and green onion and a few arugula leaves onto half of each tortilla.

4. Place folded tortillas on a parchment lined baking sheet.

5. Bake 8 to 10 minutes until edges are golden brown and cheese is melted.

6 Remove from oven using hot mitts.

7. Cut into wedges and serve with store bought salsa.

Ingredients

6 whole wheat flour tortillas
2 cups shredded cheddar or
  Monterey Jack cheese

1 cup diced cooked ham
¼ cup sliced green onions
1 cup fresh arugula
Store-bought salsa

Large mixing bowl

Small mixing bowl

Vegetable peeler

Grater

Spatula

Large spoon

Measuring spoons

Measuring cups

Apple, Carrot and Sunflower Salad

Makes 6 servings

Directions:

1. Place carrots, raisins and sunflower seeds in a large bowl.

2. Peel apple with a vegetable peeler and grate with a grater. Place apple in bowl with carrot mixture.

3. Combine orange juice and honey in a small bowl. Add mayonnaise and mix well.

4. Pour over carrot mixture; tossing gently to coat everything.

5. Refrigerate for several hours before serving for best taste.

Ingredients

2 cups shredded carrots
½ cup raisins
½ cup sunflower seeds

2 apples, peeled and grated
¼ cup orange juice
3 tablespoons honey
3 tablespoons mayonnaise

Tools

9 X 13 inch pan

Non-stick spray

Large bowl

Spatula

Large spoon

Hot mitts

Italian Brunch Casserole

Makes 8 servings

Directions:

1. Preheat oven to 350°.

2. Spray non-stick spray in a 9 x 13 inch pan.

3. Arrange French bread in bottom of pan and cover with a layer of sliced prosciutto.

4. Combine in a large bowl the parmesan cheese, fresh basil, broccoli, cottage cheese, eggs, milk, paprika and black pepper.

5. Place the mixture on top of the ham and let stand for 15 minutes.

6. Bake for 45 minutes.

7. Remove from oven using hot mitts.

8. Wait 10 minutes to cut and serve.

Ingredients

6-8 slices French bread
I cup of prosciutto Italian ham,
   thinly sliced
½ cup parmesan cheese, grated

½ cup fresh basil, chopped
½ cup chopped fresh broccoli
1-½ cups low fat cottage cheese
4 eggs

2/3 cup milk
½ teaspoon paprika
½ teaspoon black pepper

Can opener
Large bowl
Spatula
Small bowl
Measuring cups
Spoon

Shrimp, Pinto Bean and Salsa Salad

Directions:

Makes 8 servings

1. In a large bowl, combine shrimp, pinto beans, corn, celery, green onion, cilantro and cumin.

2. In a small bowl, blend salsa and apple cider vinegar.

3. Pour mixture over salad and toss well.

4. Cover and chill.

5. Serve with baked tortilla chips on the side.

Ingredients

2 cups of cooked medium-sized shrimp, shells and tails removed
1 can (15 ounces) pinto beans, rinsed and drained

1 cup frozen corn
1 ½ cups chopped celery
½ cup chopped green onion
¼ cup chopped cilantro
½ teaspoon cumin

12 ounces of store-bought salsa
¼ cup apple cider vinegar
Baked tortilla chips

25

Large non-stick
skillet

Non-stick spray

Spatula

Knife

Measuring cups

Measuring spoons

Bun-bursting Sloppy Joes

Makes 4 servings

Directions:

1. Spray a large non-stick skillet with cooking spray.

2. Cook turkey and chopped onion until cooked through and there is no pink left in the meat.

3. Add broccoli stems, salt, pepper, ketchup, sour cream, mustard, and Worcestershire sauce.

4. Heat thoroughly for several minutes and place mixture on whole wheat buns

Ingredients

1 lb of ground turkey
¼ cup chopped onion
¼ cup broccoli stems
½ teaspoon salt

¼ teaspoon black pepper
½ cup ketchup
¼ cup sour cream
2 teaspoons prepared mustard

¼ teaspoon Worcestershire
sauce
Whole wheat buns

Crunchy Pea Salad

Makes 4 servings

Directions:

1. Fry turkey bacon in skillet on stove top.

2. Drain on paper towels. Crumble bacon and set aside.

3. Combine peas, celery, green onions, sour cream, salt and pepper.

4. Toss gently to mix.

5. Before serving stir in cashews and bacon.

Ingredients

8 slices turkey bacon
1 10 ounce package
   of frozen peas, thawed

½ cup chopped celery
½ cup chopped green onions
2/3 cup sour cream

¼ teaspoon salt
¼ teaspoon black pepper
1 cup chopped cashews

Ingredients

1 teaspoon vegetable oil
½ cup chopped red onion
½ cup chopped green bell pepper
¼ teaspoon salt
¼ cup fresh basil leaves, chopped
1 teaspoon fresh rosemary, chopped

¼ teaspoon fresh oregano, chopped
¼ teaspoon black pepper
1 can (12 ounces) country-type biscuits
¼ cup shredded mozzarella cheese
½ cup spaghetti or pizza sauce
2 tablespoons grated parmesan cheese

28

Cool Calzones

Directions:

1. Preheat oven to 400°.

2. Heat the oil in a non-stick skillet over medium heat. Add onion and bell pepper. Cook and stir for 5 minutes. Remove from heat.

3. Add salt, basil, rosemary, oregano and black pepper; stir to combine. Cool slightly.

4. While onion mixture is cooling, remove biscuits from can and flatten each one into a circle about 3-4 inches and about 1/8 inch thick, using the palm of your hand.

5. Stir mozzarella into onion mixture, spoon a teaspoon of the mixture onto each biscuit. Wrap the biscuits around the filling, forming a half moon shape. Press the edges with a fork to seal; place on the baking sheet.

6. Bake 10 to 12 minutes until golden brown.

7. While calzones are baking, place spaghetti sauce in a microwave-safe dish with cover. Microwave for about 3 minutes.

8. Remove sauce from microwave using hot mitts. Remove calzones from oven using hot mitts.

9. To serve, spoon spaghetti sauce and parmesan cheese over each calzone.

Tools

Non-stick skillet
Cutting board

Large bowl
Wooden spoon
Microwave-safe dish and cover
Hot mitts

Large bowl
Strainer
Large spoon
Measuring cups
Measuring spoons

Nutritious Eggless "Egg" Salad

Makes 8 servings

Directions:

1. Drain tofu in strainer. Pat tofu dry with paper towels.

2. Combine all the ingredients in a large bowl and mix well. Mixture will not be smooth.

3. Use as a sandwich spread on whole wheat bread, adding cucumbers, lettuce, tomatoes and sprouts. It can also be used as a spread with crackers.

Ingredients

1 pound firm tofu, drained
½ cup diced celery
½ cup diced red onion

½ cup shredded carrot
1 teaspoon ground turmeric
1 teaspoon curry powder

2 teaspoons Dijon mustard

Tabouli Salad

Makes 6 servings

Tools

- Pot for boiling water
- Large bowl
- Cutting board
- Measuring cups
- Measuring spoons
- Strainer
- Mixing spoon

Directions:

1. Combine bulgur and boiling water in a large bowl.

2. Let bulgar soak for 1 hour. Using a strainer, drain off any extra water.

3. Add chopped tomatoes, green onions, parsley, garbanzo beans, olive oil, lemon juice, salt, and pepper.

4. Mix everything very thoroughly in bowl.

5. Place in refrigerator to chill for at least 2 hours or overnight.

6. When serving, place tabouli on a serving plate lined with lettuce leaves and whole olives.

Serve with pita bread torn into bite size pieces.

Ingredients

1 cup bulgur or cracked wheat
2 cups boiling water
2 medium tomatoes, diced
½ cup chopped green onions

1 cup chopped parsley
1 can garbanzo beans, rinsed
   and drained
1/3 cup extra virgin olive oil
½ cup lemon juice

1 teaspoon salt
½ teaspoon black pepper
Lettuce leaves
Black olives
Pita bread

Tempting Delicious Dinners

Tools

13 X 9 inch
  metal or glass pan

Tongs

Measuring cups

Measuring spoons

Plastic zip lock bag

Hot mitts

Oven-Fried Curry Chicken Tenders

Directions:

1. Preheat oven to 350°.

2. Melt butter in a microwave-safe dish. Set aside.

3. Combine flour, salt, pepper, paprika and curry in a zip lock bag. Shake until mixed well.

4. Place 2 or 3 chicken tenders in the bag and shake to coat with flour.

5. Place chicken in a single layer in the pan.

6. When all the chicken is in the pan, pour melted butter over the chicken.

7. Bake in the oven for 15 minutes.

8. Remove from oven using hot mitts. Serve with store-bought ranch dressing.

Ingredients

1/3 cup melted butter
½ cup all purpose flour
½ teaspoon salt

1/8 teaspoon pepper
½ teaspoon paprika
1 teaspoon curry
I lb chicken tenders
Store bought ranch dressing

Tempting Taco Salad

Makes 8 servings

Directions:

Non-stick skillet

Measuring cups

Measuring spoons

Wooden spoon

Large bowl

Small bowl

Knife

1. Cook ground beef until brown.

2. Add onions and cook for 5 minutes.

3. Drain off any grease. Place beef mixture in a large bowl.

4. Rinse and drain red beans; add to beef mixture.

5. In a small bowl combine dressing and mayonnaise together and mix well.

6. In the large bowl, combine beef mixture, dressing, lettuce, cheese, tomato, salt, pepper, and garlic powder.

7. Combine dressing and mayonnaise with the beef mixture.

8. Garnish with avocado and chips right before serving.

Ingredients

1 lb. ground beef
1 cup diced onion
1 (15 ounce) can small red beans, rinsed and drained

½ cup French dressing
½ cup mayonnaise
3 cups shredded lettuce
1 cup grated cheddar cheese
1 cup chopped tomato

½ teaspoon salt
½ teaspoon black pepper
½ teaspoon garlic powder
1 avocado, diced
Tortilla chips

Tools

Large pot for pasta

Tongs

Large bowl

Knife

Strainer for pasta

Mixing spoon

Cutting board

Hot mitts

Feta and Artichoke Pasta

Makes 6 servings

Directions:

1. Combine artichokes with the feta cheese in a large bowl. Set aside for an hour to marinate.

2. Boil pasta according to directions on package.

3. Remove pasta from pot using hot mitts.

4. Drain pasta in a strainer and place in the bowl with artichokes and feta cheese.

5. Add parsley and Parmesan cheese to the bowl, along with salt and pepper.

Ingredients

12 ounce jar of marinated artichokes
½ cup crumbled feta cheese
1 package whole wheat spaghetti
¼ cup chopped fresh parsley

2 tablespoons grated Parmesan cheese
¼ teaspoon salt
½ teaspoon pepper

Small saucepan

Skewers

Spoon

Grill

Super Pineapple Pork Kebobs

Makes 4 servings

Directions:

1. In a small saucepan, combine honey and pineapple juice and soy sauce in a small pan over low heat to make glaze.

2. Remove and set aside.

3. Thread pork cubes and bell peppers on skewers.

4. Thread remaining skewers with pineapple, banana, mandarin oranges and grapes.

5. Brush with glaze.

6. Grill or broil for about 10 minutes, basting with glaze twice.

7. Arrange kebobs on the platter with the fruit kebobs.

Glaze

1/3 cup honey

1/3 cup pineapple juice

2 tablespoons low-sodium soy sauce

Ingredients

1 pound pork loin, cut into ¾ inch cubes
1 red bell pepper, cut into chunks
1 cup canned pineapple chunks, saving juice
1 banana, cut into thick slices

1 can (11 ounces) mandarin oranges, drained
1 cup red or green grapes
12 (6 inch) skewers, soaked in water for
    30 minutes before using

Lightning Fast Lasagna

Makes 12 servings

Tools

- Large bowl
- Small bowl
- Scissors
- Measuring cups
- Measuring spoons
- 13 X 9 inch baking pan
- Aluminum foil
- Knife
- Hot mitts

Directions:

1. Preheat oven to 400°.

2. In a large bowl, combine spaghetti sauce, undrained tomatoes and water. Set aside.

3. In a small bowl, put parsley inside bowl and cut parsley into small pieces using scissors. Place egg inside bowl and whisk with parsley. Add ricotta cheese, parmesan cheese to parsley and egg. Mix well.

4. To assemble the lasagna, spread 1 ½ cups of sauce over the bottom of the pan.

5. Arrange 5 of the no boil noodles in a single layer by placing 4 noodles lengthwise and 1 noodle crosswise to cover bottom of pan.

6 Spread all the ricotta cheese mixture over the noodles. Sprinkle with half of the mozzarella cheese. Top with 1 ½ cups of sauce and remaining 5 noodles.

7. Press noodles into sauce. Spread the remaining sauce over noodles.

8. Cover with aluminum foil and bake for 45 minutes or until noodles are tender.

Ingredients

1 jar (26-28 ounces) spaghetti sauce
1 can (14 ½ ounces) diced tomatoes with basil, garlic, and oregano (do not drain)
½ cup water
¼ cup grated parmesan cheese

9. Remove lasagna using hot mitts. Uncover carefully and sprinkle remaining mozzarella cheese on top.

10. Take several basil leaves and roll them into a cigar shape. Using a knife or scissors, cut into strips and scatter on top of the lasagna.

11. Let lasagna stand 15 minutes before serving.

12. Cut into squares and serve.

¼ cup Italian flat leaf parsley
1 egg
1 container (15 ounces) ricotta cheese

2 cups shredded mozzarella cheese
Fresh basil leaves

Measuring cups

Measuring spoons

4 to 5 quart pan and lid

Wooden spoon

Can opener

Serving bowls

Kid-Friendly Easy Soup

Makes 6 to 8 servings

Directions:

1. Place pan on burner.

2. Add stewed tomatoes and chicken broth. Bring to a gentle boil over high heat, stirring with a wooden spoon.

3. Add orzo, corn, beans, carrots, oregano, and pepper to pan.

4. Reduce heat to medium low, cover and simmer for 15 minutes, stirring occasionally.

5. Turn off burner and serve soup in bowls.

Ingredients

1 can (about 14 ½ ounces) stewed tomatoes

3 cans (14 ½ ounces) low sodium

chicken broth

½ cup orzo pasta

1 package (10 ounces) frozen corn

1 package frozen cut green beans

8 ounces frozen baby carrots

1 teaspoon dry oregano

½ teaspoon pepper

Terrific Tuna Casserole

Makes 4 to 6 servings

Tools

Large bowl

Fork

4 to 5 quart pan

Strainer

Mixing spoon

Non-stick spray

2 quart casserole dish

Knife

Hot mitts

Directions:

1. Preheat oven to 350°.

2. Drain the tuna. Place tuna in a large bowl and break into small pieces with a fork. Set aside.

3. Cook the noodles according to package directions. Drain in a strainer and rinse in hot water.

4. Combine the noodles with the tuna, celery and green onions. Blend in the sour cream, mustard, mayonnaise, thyme and salt.

5. Spray non-stick spray into the casserole dish bottom and sides.

6. Spoon the mixture into the dish. Top with cheese and bake for 30 minutes or until top is golden brown.

7. Remove from oven using hot mitts.

8. Sprinkle with chopped tomato and chopped thyme.

Ingredients

2 cans (6 ½ ounces each) chunk style tuna in water
3 cups uncooked egg noodles
½ cup chopped celery

1/3 cup sliced green onions
½ cup sour cream
2 teaspoons mustard
½ cup mayonnaise
½ teaspoon dried thyme leaves
½ teaspoon salt

1 cup shredded Monterey Jack cheese
1 medium tomato, chopped
2 teaspoons fresh thyme leaves, chopped

41

Pizza Party with Everything

Directions:

Makes 6 servings

1. Preheat oven to 425°. Place parchment paper on 2 cookie sheets.

2. Stir flour, cheddar cheese, baking powder, salt, oil and milk in a medium bowl until a soft dough forms.

3. Divide the dough into 6 parts. Do not over handle the dough or the dough will get tough. Press each part into a 6 inch circle on the cookie sheet. Pinch along the sides to form an edge.

4. Spread pizza sauce over the dough, but not too thick. Top with meat and veggie toppings. Sprinkle with mozzarella cheese.

5. Bake pizzas for 10-15 minutes until crust is golden brown and cheese is melted. Remove from oven using hot mitts.

Pizzas can be made with premade shells, tortillas, muffins, pita bread and biscuits for a quick short cut.

Ingredients

1- 1/3 cups all purpose flour
½ cup shredded cheddar cheese
1 teaspoon baking powder
½ teaspoon salt

2 tablespoons vegetable oil
½ cup milk
1 jar store bought pizza sauce
2 cups sliced pepperoni, cut up ham, turkey

½ cup frozen corn, thawed and drained
¼ cup sliced olives
½ cup shredded carrots
1 cup shredded mozzarella cheese

Hawaiian Chicken Salad

Makes 2 servings

Tools

Medium size bowl

Grater

Knife

Measuring cups

Measuring spoons

Can opener

Large spoon

Directions:

1. Cut chicken into ½ inch pieces. Place in bowl.

2. Add pineapple and juice, yogurt, green onion and ginger. You do not have to peel ginger before grating.

3. Add salt and pepper. Mix well.

4. Cover and refrigerate for at least one hour to develop flavors.

Ingredients

1 ½ cups cooked chicken
1 (8 ounce) can crushed pineapple in it own juice
½ cup plain lowfat yogurt
¼ cup chopped green onion

½ teaspoon fresh ginger, grated
¼ teaspoon salt
1/8 teaspoon black pepper

Tools

- Large pot
- Knife
- Cutting board
- Can opener
- Measuring cups
- Measuring spoons
- Wooden spoon

Directions:

1. Heat olive oil in a large pot over medium heat until hot.

2. Cook onion, bell pepper, and garlic for 3 minutes, stirring constantly.

3. Add turkey and cumin; cook 3 minutes, stirring occasionally.

4. Add corn, beans, broth and cayenne pepper; bring to a simmer.

5. Simmer 10 minutes to blend flavors.

Ingredients

1 tablespoon olive oil
1 medium onion, halved and sliced
½ cup medium yellow bell pepper, chopped into ½ inch pieces

2 cloves garlic, minced
2 cups shredded cooked turkey or ham
1 tablespoon ground cumin
1 ½ cups frozen roasted corn

1 (15 or 19 ounce) can canellini beans, not drained
1 (14 ounce) can low-sodium chicken broth
¼ teaspoon cayenne pepper

Quinoa with Watermelon and Feta

Makes 4 servings

Tools

- Saucepan
- Strainer
- Knife
- Cutting board
- Whisk
- Large bowl
- Small bowl
- Measuring cups
- Measuring spoons

Directions:

1. Rinse quinoa in water using a mesh container.

2. Place coconut milk in saucepan and bring to simmer.

3. Add drained quinoa, simmer and cover until liquid is absorbed, about 15 minutes. When finished, fluff quinoa with a fork and set aside.

4. Place spinach, feta, watermelon and onions in a large bowl.

5. Cut limes and juice into a small bowl. Whisk with olive oil, salt and pepper.

6. Add quinoa to the large bowl, add dressing and mix thoroughly.

Ingredients

1 cup of quinoa grain
1 ½ cups light coconut milk
1 bag of baby spinach
½ cup feta cheese

2 cups watermelon cut in medium chunks
¼ cup red onion, sliced

Dressing:
2 limes, juiced
1/3 cup extra virgin olive oil
¼ teaspoon salt
1/8 teaspoon black pepper

45

Can opener
Strainer
Casserole dish
Measuring cups
Measuring spoons
Large spoon
Knife
Cutting board
Grater
Hot mitts

Tropical Baked Beans

Makes 4 servings

Directions:

1. Preheat oven to 375°.

2. Rinse and drain the beans. Drain pineapple.

3. In a 1 or 2 quart casserole dish, mix beans, pineapple, barbecue sauce, onions, sugar, lime juice, grated ginger and mustard. The ginger does not have to be peeled before being grated.

4. Bake bean mixture, uncovered, for about 25 minutes, or until bubbling in the center. Remove beans using hot mitts.

5. Slice green onions and use as garnish on top of the beans.

Ingredients

1 can (about 15 ounces) black beans, drained and rinsed
1 can (about 15 ounces) red kidney beans, drained and rinsed
1 can (8 ounces) crushed pineapple in unsweetened juice, drained
½ cup tomato-based barbeque sauce

½ cup chopped green onions
1/3 cup firmly packed brown sugar
2 tablespoons lime juice
1 tablespoon fresh grated ginger
2 teaspoons dry mustard
Whole green onions for garnish

Asian Spinach Salad

Makes 4 servings

Tools

- Can opener
- Whisk
- Measuring cups
- Measuring spoons
- Knife
- Small bowl
- Large bowl
- Non-stick skillet
- Strainer
- Grater

Directions:

1. Combine and whisk together oil, vinegar, and honey in a small bowl.

2. Grate the ginger using a grater. The ginger does not have to be peeled before being grated. Place ginger in bowl, along with mustard, sesame oil and salt. Set aside.

3. Combine spinach, oranges, cucumbers, mushrooms, and green onions in a large bowl.

4. Put almonds in a non-stick pan and toast for 2 minutes. Place in large bowl with salad.

5. Toss with dressing just before serving. Garnish with chow mein noodles.

All the ingredients may be found in a regular supermarket.

Ingredients

Dressing:
3 tablespoons vegetable oil
3 tablespoons rice vinegar
2 teaspoons honey
2 teaspoons grated fresh ginger

1 teaspoon Dijon mustard
¼ teaspoon sesame oil
¼ teaspoon salt
Salad:
8 cups baby spinach
1 can (11 ounces) mandarin oranges, drained

¼ cup cucumber, thinly sliced
½ cup button mushrooms, thinly sliced
¼ cup sliced green onions
½ cup sliced almonds, toasted
½ cup chow mein noodles

Pasta pot

Strainer

Wooden spoon

Tongs

Large bowl

Hot mitts

Speedy Spaghetti with Fresh Tomato Sauce

Makes 6 servings

Directions:

1. Boil spaghetti in large pot according to package directions.

2. Combine the tomatoes, onion, garlic, basil, olive oil, salt and pepper in a large bowl.

3. When the spaghetti is done, remove from stove using hot mitts and drain in strainer. Do not rinse.

4. Toss the sauce with the hot pasta and serve with grated parmesan cheese.

Ingredients

1 package whole wheat spaghetti
No Bake Sauce:
4 ripe medium size tomatoes, chopped

1 cup chopped red onion
2 cloves garlic, minced
4 tablespoons fresh basil, minced
2/3 cup extra virgin olive oil

½ teaspoon salt
¼ teaspoon black pepper
½ cup grated parmesan cheese

Confetti Vegetable Rice

Makes 6 servings

Directions:

1. Preheat oven to 350°.

2. Spray non-stick spray in baking pan.

3. Combine rice, garlic salt, broccoli, bell pepper, milk, eggs, nutmeg and Worcestershire sauce in baking pan.

4. Put cheese on top of the rice mixture and place pieces of butter on top.

5. Cover with foil and bake for 1 hour.

6. Remove from oven using hot mitts.

Ingredients

1½ cups cooked white rice
½ teaspoon garlic salt
1 package frozen broccoli, thawed and drained

1 medium red bell pepper, diced small
3 cups milk
2 eggs
¼ teaspoon nutmeg

1 teaspoon Worcestershire sauce
1 cup grated cheddar cheese
4 tablespoons butter

49

Cheesy Italian Chicken Veggie Packets

Makes 6 servings

Tools

Non-stick cooking spray

2 large baking sheets

Aluminum foil

Knife

Measuring cups

Measuring spoons

Hot mitts

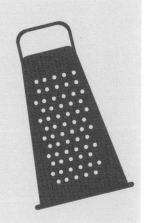

Directions:

1. Preheat oven to 450°.

2. Set out 2 large baking sheets. Take aluminum foil and make six 12 x 10 sheets. Spray non-stick spray on foil.

3. Place a chicken tender on one half, about 3 inches from the short side. Top with ¼ cup of sauce, ½ cup zucchini, ¼ cup corn, 2 tablespoons mushrooms, and ¼ cup cheese.

4. Fold edges and seal securely, place 3 on baking sheet. Repeat, making 6 packets total.

5. Bake for 30 minutes.

6. Remove from the oven using hot mitts and let stand for a few minutes before opening.

7. Slide contents of each packet onto a plate. Place basil on top and serve.

Ingredients

6 medium-sized uncooked boneless chicken tender pieces
1 ½ cups (26 ounces) spaghetti sauce
3 cups thinly sliced zucchini

1 can (11 ounces) corn, drained and rinsed
1 cup sliced fresh mushrooms
1 ½ cups shredded mozzarella cheese
½ cup fresh basil, sliced

First, place a chicken tender on one half, about 3 inches from the short side.

Then, top with ¼ cup of sauce, ½ cup zucchini, ¼ cup corn, 2 tablespoons mushrooms, and ¼ cup cheese.

Finally, fold edges and seal securely.

Dazzling Desserts

Dirt Dessert with Gummy Worms

Makes 6 servings

Directions:

1. Place the cookies in a food processor and pulse until grated. Set aside.

2. In a large bowl, combine the three pudding mixes with the milk. Add the entire container of Cool Whip® to the pudding mixture and beat at low speed for 3 minutes.

3. In a large bowl, combine the three pudding mixes with the milk.

Add the entire container of Cool Whip® to the pudding mixture and beat at low speed for 3 minutes.

4. Stick gummy worm candies out of the top of the "dirt."

Variations:

Use chocolate pudding and a clean flowerpot. Freeze finished product and use as a centerpiece while dining. Garnish the top of the "dirt" with edible flowers, such as nasturtiums. Eat the centerpiece after it has thawed.

Ingredients

1 package chocolate sandwich cookies, grated
3 small (3 ounces each) packages of instant vanilla pudding
5 cups milk, (more may be added as necessary)
1 medium (8 ounces) non-dairy whipped topping
Gummy worm candies

Molasses Cookies

Makes 4 dozen

Non-stick spray

Large bowl

Medium bowl

Measuring cups

Measuring spoons

Electric mixer

Knife

Baking sheets

Mixing spoon

Tablespoon

Wire Rack

Hot mitts

Directions:

1. Preheat oven to 350°. Spray baking sheets with non-stick spray.

2. In a large bowl, by hand, stir together flour, salt, baking soda, ginger, cloves and cinnamon.

3. In another large bowl, use the electric beater on medium speed to beat butter, shortening and sugar until light and fluffy.

4. Add in molasses. Add eggs, one at a time, beating well after each addition. Gradually beat in flour mixture and mix well.

5. Form dough into 1-½ inch ball and place on baking sheet. Place several slices of ginger on ball and flatten with bottom of a glass.

6. Bake cookies for 12 minutes or until puffed and golden brown.

7. Remove from oven using hot mitts and place on wire rack to cool.

Ingredients

4 cups all purpose flour
½ teaspoon salt
2-¼ teaspoons baking soda
2 teaspoons ground ginger

1-¼ teaspoon ground cloves
1 tablespoon cinnamon
½ cup unsalted butter,
   room temperature
½ cup vegetable shortening

1 ½ cups sugar
1 cup brown sugar
½ cup molasses
2 eggs
¼ cup crystallized ginger,
   diced small

Measuring cups

Measuring spoons

Knife

2 microwave-safe
bowls

Medium-sized bowl

Spoons

6 serving bowls

Farmers Market Fruits with Yummy Sauces

Makes 6 servings

Directions:

1. Slice fruit and place in a medium-sized bowl.

2. In separate microwave-safe bowls, warm the caramel sauce for about 20 seconds.

3. For the peanut butter sauce, combine the marshmallow cream, peanut butter, lime juice and water in a small bowl. Whisk until everything is well blended.

4. Divide the fruits between six plates and serve with the two sauces.

Ingredients

2 cups sliced bananas
2 cups sliced peaches
2 cups sliced apricots

2 cups sliced nectarines
1 cup store bought caramel sauce

Peanut Butter Sauce:
½ cup marshmallow cream
¼ cup creamy peanut butter
1 teaspoon lime juice
1 teaspoons water

Large bowl

Wooden spoon

Measuring cups

Measuring spoons

Knife

Teaspoon

Baking sheets

Hot mitts

Oat Chewy Cookies

Makes 3 dozen

Directions:

1. Preheat oven to 350°.

2. Mix flour, oats, baking soda, cinnamon and nutmeg in a large bowl.

3. Combine eggs, butter and honey, mix until well blended. Add the flour mixture.

4. Stir in carrots, apricots, dates, cranberries and cereal.

5. Drop the dough by rounded teaspoonful on an ungreased cookie sheet, two inches apart.

6. Remove cookies using hot mitts and place on wire rack to cool.

Ingredients

1 cup all purpose flour
1 cup rolled oats
½ teaspoon baking soda
¾ teaspoon cinnamon
¾ teaspoon nutmeg

2 eggs
¼ cup unsalted butter, melted
½ cup honey
1 cup shredded carrots
1 cup dried apricots, chopped

1 cup pitted dates, chopped
1 cup dried cranberries
1 ½ cups oat circles cereal

Tools

Medium size bowl

Measuring cups

Measuring spoons

Pastry blender or
2 knives

Non-stick spray

13 x 9 inch baking
pan

Mixing bowl

Electric mixer

Spatula

Hot mitts

Wire rack

Lemon Coconut Bars

Makes 3 dozen

Directions:

1. Preheat oven to 350°.

2. Combine flour and confectioners' sugar in a medium size bowl. Cut in the butter using pastry blender or two knives until dough is crumbly.

3. Lightly spray the pan with non-stick spray. Press dough into the bottom of the baking pan.

4. Bake for 15 minutes. Remove using hot mitts.

5. In a mixing bowl, beat the eggs and sugar.

6. Grate the lemon with a grater, making sure to only grate the yellow part of the lemon. Add lemon zest, lemon juice and baking powder into the mixing bowl. Mix well.

7. Pour over the crust. Sprinkle coconut evenly over the top.

8. Bake for 20-25 minutes until golden brown.

9. Remove pan using hot mitts. Cool on a wire rack. Cut into bars.

Ingredients

1-½ cups all purpose flour
½ cup confectioners' sugar
¾ cup cold unsalted butter
4 eggs

1 cup of sugar
½ cup lemon juice
1 teaspoon lemon zest
1 teaspoon baking powder
¾ cup unsweetened flaked coconut

Peanut Butter Fingers

Makes 3 dozen

Directions:

1. Preheat oven to 350°.

2. For frosting, combine peanut butter, sugar and milk. Blend to smooth and set aside.

3. For bars, combine butter, sugars, egg, peanut butter, baking soda, vanilla, salt, flour and rolled oats in a large bowl.

4. Place ingredients into baking pan and bake for 15 minutes.

5. Remove from oven using hot mitts. Turn off oven.

6. Sprinkle the bag of chocolate chips on top of the mixture. Drizzle frosting over chips and spread like icing. Return the pan to the oven for a few minutes to melt the chips.

7. Remove from oven using hot mitts. Cut into bars when cooled.

Ingredients

½ cup unsalted butter, melted
½ cup sugar
½ cup brown sugar
1 egg
1/3 cup smooth peanut butter

1 teaspoon baking soda
1 teaspoon vanilla extract
¼ teaspoon salt
1 cup flour
1 cup rolled oats
1 small (6 ounces) package

chocolate chips, milk or
   dark chocolate
Frosting:
¼ cup smooth peanut butter
½ cup confectioners' sugar
3 tablespoons milk

Tools

Medium bowl
Large bowl
Measuring cups
Measuring spoons
Wooden spoon
Spatula
Baking pan
Hot mitts
Scissors

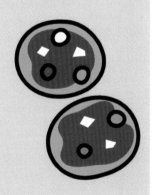

Decorated Pizza Cookies

Makes 12 cookies

Directions:

1. Preheat oven to 350°

2. In a medium bowl, mix flour, oats, baking soda and salt. Set bowl aside.

3. In a large bowl, beat butter and brown sugar until creamy. Add egg and vanilla and beat well.

4. Add flour mixture to butter and mix well. Stir in chocolate chips. Shape the dough into one ball, using floured hands. Divide dough into 10 or 12 pieces and shape into individual cookies. Place on an ungreased baking pan.

5. Cook for 10-12 minutes until light golden brown.

6. Remove from oven using hot mitts and let cookies cool completely.

7. Spread cooled cookies with frosting. To decorate, cut gumdrops into pieces using scissors. Top cookies with gumdrops, chocolate pieces, chopped up candy bar.

Ingredients

1 cup all purpose flour
¾ cup oats
½ teaspoon baking soda
¼ teaspoon salt

½ cup (1 stick) unsalted butter, room temperature
½ cup packed brown sugar
1 egg
½ teaspoon vanilla
1 cup semi-sweet chocolate chips

1 cup prepared milk chocolate frosting (the kind in the can)
Gumdrops, candy-coated chocolate pieces and a white chocolate bar

Fabulous Fruit Kebobs

Makes 8 servings

Directions:

1. Drain the canned fruits, keeping ¼ cup of the pineapple syrup. Set aside.

2. Cut apples, pears and kiwis into chunks.

3. Thread the bamboo skewer with all the different fruits. Refrigerate until ready to serve.

4. Use a whisk to blend together cream cheese, cinnamon and pineapple syrup to make the dipping sauce. Refrigerate until ready to use.

5. Chop walnuts and toast in a dry pan for 3 minutes on the stove. Remove and place in a small bowl.

6. Serve fruit kebobs on a platter, surrounded by bowls of the cream cheese dip, chocolate syrup, chopped nuts and coconut.

Can opener

Bamboo skewers

Strainer

Measuring cups

Measuring spoons

Large bowl

2 small bowls

Whisk

Skillet

Knife

Cutting board

Platter

Small bowls for dips

Ingredients

2 large apples cut into thick slices

1 can (8 ounces) sliced pears, in light syrup

1 can (8 ounces) pineapple chunks, in light syrup

4 kiwi, peeled and cut into chunks

8 (8 inch) bamboo skewers

Dip:

1 cup of strawberry whipped cream cheese

½ teaspoon cinnamon

1 cup toasted walnuts, finely chopped

1 cup sweetened flaked coconut

1 cup chocolate syrup

Large bowl

Small knife

Pastry blender

Measuring cups

9 inch square
baking pan

Hot mitts

Spatula

**Blueberries are
considered the
perfect food!**

Ooey Gooey Berry Bars

Makes 16 bars

Directions:

1. Preheat oven to 375°.

2. In a large bowl, mix flours, oats and brown sugar with a pastry blender.

3. Cut butter into small pieces using a knife and add to the flour mixture. Using the pastry blender, mix butter until the mixture is crumbly.

4. Measure out 1 cup of crumb mixture and set aside for the topping. Press the remaining mixture onto the bottom of a 9 inch square pan.

5. Spread the preserves over the crust. Sprinkle with blueberries. Sprinkle the remaining crumb mixture evenly over the blueberries.

6. Bake for 30-35 minutes until golden brown. Remove from pan using hot mitts.

7. When cooled, cut into squares and remove from pan with a spatula.

Ingredients

1 cup all purpose flour
½ cup wheat flour
1 ¼ cups oats
½ cup packed brown sugar

¾ cup (1 ½ sticks) unsalted butter
½ raspberry or strawberry preserves
1 cup fresh or frozen blueberries

Mango Sticky Rice

Makes 4 servings

Tools

Large bowl

Small bowl

Can opener

Strainer

Measuring cups

Measuring spoons

Small knife

Cutting board

Directions:

1. Cook rice in water according to directions. Let cool and transfer to a bowl.

2. Mix coconut milk and brown sugar together, pour over rice.

3. Add mango and mix well.

4. Spoon into serving bowls and sprinkle with crystallized ginger.

5. Serve chilled or room temperature.

Ingredients

1 cup jasmine rice

¾ cup canned coconut milk

¼ cup packed brown sugar

2 cans (8 ounces each) of mangoes, drained and sliced

2 tablespoons finely chopped crystallized ginger

Speedy Orange Cake

Makes 8 servings

Measuring cups

Measuring spoons

Large bowl

Small bowl

9 x 9 baking dish

Non-stick cooking spray

Can opener

Grater

Spatula

Hot mitts

Mixing spoons

Wire rack

Directions:

1. Preheat oven to 325°. Spray baking dish with cooking spray.

2. In a large bowl, combine eggs, vegetable oil, pineapple, orange juice together for 1 minute.

3. Add cinnamon, carrots, nuts and flour and stir for 2 minutes.

4. Add baking powder and soda, stir for 30 seconds.

5. Pour immediately into a 9 x 9 baking dish. Bake for 35 minutes.

6. Remove carefully from oven using hot mitts. Place cake on a wire rack to cool.

7. Mix the cream cheese with honey in a small bowl.

8. Using a spatula, spread icing on top of cake. Decorate with cut orange slices.

Ingredients

3 eggs
½ cup vegetable oil
1 can (20 ounces) crushed pineapple with juice
¼ cup orange juice concentrate

½ teaspoon cinnamon
1 cup shredded carrots
1 cup walnut pieces
2 cups flour
2 teaspoons baking soda

1 teaspoon baking powder
Icing:
1 cup cream cheese
2 teaspoons honey
1 orange, cut into slices

Brownies Galore

Heavy saucepan

8 inch square baking pan

Non-stick cooking spray

Wooden spoon

Measuring cups

Measuring spoons

Directions:

1. Preheat oven to 350°. Spray 8 inch baking pan with non-stick spray.

2. Melt the chocolate in a small saucepan over low heat, stirring constantly. Stir in the syrup.

3. Remove the pan from the heat and add the butter. Beat until the mixture is smooth.

4. Stir in the vanilla and eggs and mix thoroughly.

5. In a small bowl, stir together the sugar, salt and flour. Add this to the chocolate mixture and blend thoroughly.

6. Pour batter into the baking pan and bake for 30 minutes.

7. Remove from oven using hot mitts and place on wire rack to cool.

8. Allow the brownies to cool completely in the pan; cut into squares before serving.

Ingredients

6 ounces semi sweet chocolate, chopped
¼ cup chocolate syrup
½ cup unsalted butter, room temperature
1 teaspoon vanilla

2 eggs, lightly beaten
¾ cup granulated sugar
1/8 teaspoon salt
½ cup all purpose flour

Nutty Zucchini Pumpkin Bread

Makes 1 loaf

Tools

2 Large bowls

Grater

Spatula

Measuring cups

Measuring spoons

Loaf pan, 9 x 5 x 3 inches

Non-stick spray

Wire Rack

Hot mitts

Directions:

1. Preheat oven to 350°. Spray non-stick spray in a 9 x 5 inch loaf pan. Set aside.

2. In a large bowl, combine pumpkin, zucchini, sugar, eggs, oil, butter and vanilla. Mix thoroughly.

3. In the other large bowl, combine flour, baking soda, baking powder, salt, cinnamon and pumpkin pie spice.

4. Add the dry ingredients to the pumpkin batter, mixing flour until barely moistened. Stir in the pecan pieces.

5. Put batter into baking pan and bake for 1 hour or until a wooden toothpick inserted into the center comes out clean.

6 Remove bread from oven using hot mitts. Cool for 15 minutes.

7. Remove the bread from the baking pan and let it cool on a wire rack.

Ingredients

1 cup pumpkin
1 cup grated zucchini
¾ cup sugar
2 eggs

¼ cup vegetable oil
¼ unsalted butter, melted
1 teaspoon vanilla
2 cups all purpose flour
1 teaspoon baking soda

½ teaspoon baking powder
¼ teaspoon salt
1 teaspoon ground cinnamon
1 teaspoon pumpkin pie spice
½ cup pecan pieces

Tools

Medium bowl

Cutting board

Knife

Measuring cups

Measuring spoons

Electric mixer

Spatula

Banana Split Pie

Makes 6 servings

Directions:

1. Take plastic top off crust.

2. Slice bananas; lay on top of the crust, alternating with strawberry jam and chocolate sauce until they are all used up.

3. With an electric mixer, on high speed, whip heavy cream, sugar and vanilla together until stiff peaks form.

4. Spread softened ice cream over on top of banana, strawberry and chocolate mixture. Next spread the whipping cream mixture.

5. Garnish with chopped walnuts or pecans. Place in freezer for at least one hour.

6. Remove from freezer 15 minutes before serving.

Ingredients

1 9 -inch store bought graham cracker crust
2 bananas, sliced lengthwise into several slices
1 ½ pints of Neapolitan ice cream, softened
½ cups strawberry jam

¼ cup chocolate or fudge sauce
1 cup heavy cream
2 tablespoons sugar
1 teaspoon vanilla extract
¼ cup chopped walnuts or pecans

Super Healthy Snacks

Food processor

Can opener

Strainer

Measuring cups

Small oven-proof dish

Mixing spoon

Hot mitts

Hot Cheddar Bean Dip

Makes 2-1/2 cups

Directions:

1. Preheat oven to 350°.

2. Place all the ingredients into a food processor.

3. Pulse until all the ingredients are blended together.

4. Spoon into an oven-proof dish.

5. Bake for 30 minutes until bubbly.

6. Remove from oven using hot mitts.

7. Serve with whole wheat or rice crackers.

Ingredients

½ cup low fat mayonnaise
1 can (16 ounce) pinto beans, rinsed and drained
1 cup shredded cheddar cheese
1 can (4 ounces) chopped green chilies

Baking dish

Food processor

Can opener

Knife

Measuring cups

Measuring spoons

Spatula

Platter

Hot mitts s

Layered Mediterranean Dip

Makes 8 servings

Directions:

1. Preheat oven to 350°.

2. Place pita on baking dish and toast in the oven for 10 minutes.

3. Remove from oven using hot mitts. Cut pita into wedges.

4. Place sour cream, milk, beans, garlic, cumin and salt in a food processor.

5. Pulse until well blended. If mixture seems too thick, add more milk by the tablespoon.

6. Spread hummus on a platter, arrange toppings over and serve with toasted pita chips.

Ingredients

Hummus:
1 cup light sour cream
¼ cup skim milk
1 (15 ounce) can garbanzo beans, rinsed and drained

2 teaspoons finely chopped fresh garlic
½ teaspoon cumin
½ teaspoon salt
Toppings for Hummus:
½ cup plain non fat yogurt
¼ cup diced cucumber

¼ cup chopped tomato
2 tablespoons finely chopped red onion
¼ cup crumbled feta cheese
2 tablespoons chopped parsley
Whole wheat pita bread

Tools

Non-stick spray

Large bowl

Knife

Measuring cups

Measuring spoons

Mixing spoon

Muffin pan

Hot mitts

Prosciutto and Pesto Biscuits

Makes 20 biscuits

Directions:

1. Preheat oven to 350°.

2. Spray non-stick spray into muffin cup pan.

3. In a large bowl, combine prosciutto, cheese, tomato, mayonnaise and pesto sauce.

4. Cut each biscuit in half. Place biscuit halves into greased muffin cup pan, pressing gently to fit.

5. Spoon 1 tablespoon of filling into each cup, making sure you do not put too much in each one.

6. Bake for 20 to 25 minutes.

7. Remove from oven using hot mitts.

8. Serve biscuits warm.

Ingredients

½ cup cut up prosciutto ham
½ cup shredded Swiss cheese
1 small tomato, chopped

½ cup low fat mayonnaise
1 tablespoons store bought pesto sauce
1 package (10 ounces) refrigerated flaky biscuits

Cheesy Oven Fries

Makes 4-6 servings

Cutting board

Large bowl

Baking sheet

Non-stick spray

Microwave-safe dish

Knife

Directions:

1. Preheat oven to 375°. Spray non-stick spray on baking sheet.

2. Wash potatoes well, and cut each into 8 wedges; set aside.

3. Combine parmesan cheese, salt, garlic powder, and paprika in a shallow pan, stirring well.

4. Microwave butter in a microwave-safe dish.

5. Dip potato wedges in melted butter; arrange in a single layer on baking sheet. Sprinkle cheese mixture evenly over potatoes.

6. Bake, uncovered, for 40 minutes or until potatoes are tender and browned.

7. Remove potatoes from oven using hot mitts.

Ingredients

3 medium potatoes
1/3 cup parmesan cheese, grated
½ teaspoon salt

¾ teaspoon garlic powder
¾ teaspoon paprika
3 tablespoon unsalted butter, melted

Nutty Carrot Spread

Makes 2-1/2 cups

Directions:

1. Combine all the ingredients in a small bowl.

2. Use as a sandwich spread with whole wheat bread or serve as a snack on top of celery sticks.

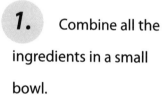

Ingredients

1 cup shredded carrots
1 cup creamy peanut butter
½ cup raisins
2 tablespoons honey

Party Popcorn

Directions:

1. Microwave popcorn according to the package directions. Pour popcorn into large serving bowl.

2. Melt butter in a microwave-safe container. Add parmesan cheese and salt to melted butter and pour over popcorn.

Ingredients

1 bag microwave light popcorn
1/3 cup melted unsalted butter
¼ cup parmesan cheese
¼ teaspoon salt

Large bowl
Food processor
Knife
Brush
Microwave-safe dish
Baking sheet
Hot mitts

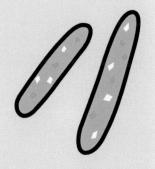

Quick Garlic Sticks

Makes 20 sticks

Directions:

1. Preheat oven to 350°.

2. Combine square-shaped cereal with garlic powder and salt in food processor. Pulse to crush square-shaped cereal and mix ingredients.

3. Place butter in a microwave-safe dish and microwave for 30 seconds to melt butter. Add butter to food processor and pulse.

4. Cut each biscuit in half. Roll between palms of hands into sticks 8 inches long.

5. Brush each stick with remaining melted butter. Coat with the square-shaped cereal mix.

6. Place sticks on the baking sheet and bake for 7 minutes until golden brown.

7. Remove from oven using hot mitts. Serve warm.

Ingredients

2 cups rice, wheat or corn
   square-shaped cereal
1 teaspoon garlic powder

½ teaspoon salt
4 tablespoons unsalted butter, melted
1 package refrigerated biscuits

Tools

- Skillet
- Baking sheet
- Aluminum foil
- Spatula
- Measuring cups
- Wooden spoon
- Hot mitts

Tiny Tacos

Makes 8 servings

Directions:

1. Preheat oven to 350°.

2. Prepare taco seasoning mixture according to directions on package with meat and water.

3. Stir in 2/3 cup of fried onions, green chilies and chopped tomato.

4. Arrange the tortilla chips on a foil lined baking sheet. Spread each chip with 1 tablespoon meat mixture.

5. Sprinkle evenly with cheese and remaining onions.

6. Bake for 5 minutes until cheese melts and onions are golden.

7. Remove from oven using hot mitts.

8. Garnish with chopped cilantro. Serve immediately.

Ingredients

1 pound ground turkey
1 package of taco seasoning mix
¾ cup water
1 cup fried onions, divided use

1 can (4 ounces) green chilies
1 small tomato, chopped
1/3 cup shredded cheddar
  cheese 1/3

½ cup chopped cilantro
32 bite size tortilla chips
  (tortilla chips shaped like a
  bowl work really well)

Pretzel Mania

Tools

Small bowl
Baking sheet
Non-stick spray
Pastry brush
Pan with water
Hot mitts

For a variation, combine ¼ cup sugar and 2 tablespoons cinnamon and sprinkle over pretzels instead of salt.

Directions:

1. Thaw frozen bread dough overnight in refrigerator.

2. Preheat oven to 350°. Spray non-stick spray on baking sheet.

3. Divide each thawed bread dough loaf into 12 balls.

4. Using your hands, roll each ball into a rope about 12 inches long. Shape dough into pretzels by forming a knot and looping the ends through.

5. After forming pretzel, place it on the baking sheet, one inch apart from the other pretzels.

6. In a small bowl combine the egg white and water. Brush the pretzels and sprinkle salt on top.

7. In a large shallow pan pour one inch of hot water and place it on the bottom rack of the oven. This will provide moist heat while the pretzels cook.

8. Place the baking sheet with pretzels on the middle rack of the oven. Bake for 20 minutes until golden brown.

9. Serve the pretzels with mustard as a sauce.

Ingredients

2 loaves frozen whole wheat bread (thawed)
1 egg white, slightly beaten

1 teaspoon water
Sea salt

Cinnamon Pita Chips with Fruit Salsa

Makes 24 chips

Directions:

1. Preheat oven to 375°. Stack pita bread on top of one another and cut into 8 pieces with a knife.

2. Place the butter in a microwave-safe dish and microwave for about 30 seconds.

3. Combine sugar and cinnamon in a small bowl and set aside.

4. Brush the melted butter onto the pita chip. Place chips on a baking sheet. Sprinkle with the sugar and cinnamon mix. Bake the pita chips for 8 minutes.

5. While chips bake, pour the pineapple with the juice into a small mixing bowl. Dice the apple and banana with a knife and add to the bowl. Stir the contents of the bowl to mix thoroughly. Peel the kiwi with a knife, dice and add it to the bowl. Stir to mix well.

6. Remove chips from oven using hot mitts. Serve chips and salsa immediately.

Ingredients

Chips:
3 pieces pita bread rounds
3 tablespoons unsalted butter
2 tablespoons sugar

1 teaspoon ground cinnamon
Salsa:
1 can of crushed pineapple in juice

1 small tart apple, Gala or Granny Smith
½ ripe banana
½ cup kiwi

Blender
Measuring cups
Measuring spoons

Orange Vanilla Blender Blast

Makes 4 servings

Directions:

1. Add ice to blender.

2. Next add orange juice concentrate, milk, water, sugar and vanilla. Make sure the surface of the ice is just covered. If there is not enough liquid, add a little water.

3. Cover blender tightly, hold on and blend or crush to smooth the ingredients.

4. Pour into glasses and serve immediately.

Ingredients

1 6-ounce can frozen orange juice concentrate
½ cup milk
½ cup water

¼ cup sugar
½ teaspoon vanilla extract
5 or 6 ice cubes

About the Author

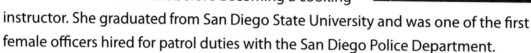

 Janet Burgess is a native San Diegan who had a long career in law enforcement before becoming a cooking instructor. She graduated from San Diego State University and was one of the first female officers hired for patrol duties with the San Diego Police Department.

 Janet finished culinary school in 1998 and studied in Tuscany, Italy, as well as The Culinary Institute of America. She then opened her own school, **4littlecooks**® Hands-on Cooking School, specializing in healthy cooking classes for children. She also taught for many years at the Macy's School of Cooking where she developed the Iron Chef Competition series.

 In addition to teaching, she does food styling for clients. Her food and table settings have appeared on ABC, NBC and CBS. Janet's recipes have been featured in the San Diego Union Tribune and the Los Angeles Times.

 Janet is a founding member of Les Dames d'Escoffier International, San Diego Chapter, a non-profit worldwide organization of women leaders of achievement in the culinary, beverage and hospitality professions.

Appendix

Author Janet Burgess' favorite books

- Food Lover's Companion by Sharon Tyler Herbst (Barron's Educational Series, Inc, 2001)
- Cooking with Les Dames d'Escoffier (Sasquatch Books, 2008)
- How to Cook Everything by Mark Bittman (Simon & Schuster Macmillan Company)

Author Janet Burgess' favorite websites:

- www.epicurious.com
- www.goldminenaturalfoods.com
- www.kingarthurflour.com
- www.penzeys.com
- www.fantes.com
- www.LDEI.org

Author Janet Burgess' cooking school

4littlecooks® Hands-on Cooking School
4littlecooks@gmail.com
www.4littlecooks.com
Facebook: 4littlecooks®
Twitter:@4littlecooks®

McKinley Elementary School
McKinley School Foundation of San Diego
A portion of the proceeds of this book will go to the Foundation at McKinley Elementary School
in San Diego to help fund their Octopuses Garden Project which benefits all students.

Fun, Fast & Fresh Recipes for Young Chefs

Have you been looking for fun, fast, fresh and easy recipes to make with your children?
CHOP, COOK, MUNCH! is for you!

- Spend quality time with your children teaching them how to cook and have fun using simple ingredients.

- More than 60 irresistible mouth watering recipes for kids to enjoy.

- Kid pleasing recipes for breakfast, lunch, dinner, dessert and snacks in 30 minutes or less.

- Chock full of favorite, amazing kid tested recipes, tips, a tool list and everything your child needs to know to be a cool chef.

- Share healthy and time saving recipes with your children.

Teach fresh and creative meals your children will love to make with you.

Author Janet Burgess is launching **4littlecooks**® classes and releasing her new cookbook, CHOP, COOK, MUNCH! so children can learn fun, fast and fresh recipes for cooking and sharing. CHOP, COOK, MUNCH! is one of the very few cookbooks for young chefs between ages 5-13.

Have fun sharing these kid-tested recipes with your child or children…
In fact, invite your friends and neighbors for a **4littlecooks**® party and share with everyone!

Janet has taught children's cooking classes since 1998. She was the first in the United States to bring the Iron Chef Competition concept to children's cooking classes at the Macy's School of Cooking. Janet's passion has always been to provide easy healthy recipes and tips for parents to share with their children.

CPSIA information can be obtained
at www.ICGtesting.com
Printed in the USA
LVIW012338110612

285686LV00001B

9 781477 204290